Running Races

Debbie Croft
Photographs by Lindsay Edwards

Contents

Goal

To run in a short race and in a long race

Equipment

You will need:

- a coach with a whistle
- a short running track with **lanes**
- a long running track around a field

Steps for the Short Race

1. Stand with your feet behind the start line.

2. Wait for the coach to blow the whistle.

3. Start to run.

Run as fast as you can.

Do not look behind you.

4. Run with your arms bent.
Move your arms
in time with your legs
so you can run faster.

5. Stay in your lane
for the whole race.

6. Run right up to the **tape**
at the end of the lane
before you slow down.

Steps for the Long Race

1. Go to your start lane. Stand behind the line.

2. Wait for the coach to blow the whistle.

3. Start to run,
   but do not run too fast
   at first.
   Stay in your start lane.

4. Move to the left lane
   when you get
   to the green **flag**.
   Be careful not to
   trip up other runners
   in the race.

5. Start to run faster now.
Look out for runners
who may be coming
past you.

6. Run as fast as you can
to the flags
at the end of the race.

Glossary

flag

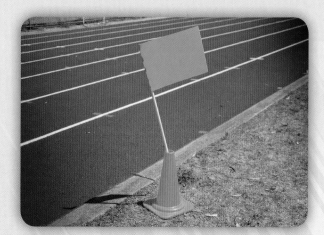

lanes

tape